IT'S COOL TO LEARN ABOUT COUNTRIES

Social Studies Explorer

# JAPAN

➦ by Barbara A. Somervill

CHERRY LAKE PUBLISHING • ANN ARBOR, MICHIGAN

Published in the United States of America
by Cherry Lake Publishing
Ann Arbor, Michigan
www.cherrylakepublishing.com

Content Adviser: Daniel C. O'Neill, PhD, Department of East Asian Languages and Cultures,
University of California, Berkeley

Book design: The Design Lab

Photo credits: Cover and page 1, ©MeeRok/Shutterstock, Inc.; cover stamp, ©iStockphoto.com/raclro; page
4, ©Hiroshi Ichikawa/Shutterstock, Inc.; page 5, ©Mike Tan C. T./Shutterstock, Inc.; page 7, ©Amy Nichole
Harris/Shutterstock, Inc.; page 9, ©Craig Hanson/Shutterstock, Inc.; page 11, ©kkaplin/Shutterstock, Inc.;
page 12, ©melissaf84/Shutterstock, Inc.; pages 13 and 21, ©jeremy sutton-hibbert/Alamy; page 14, ©JTB
Photo Communications, Inc./Alamy; page 15, ©iStockphoto.com/travelphotographer; page 16, ©Lim Yong
Hian/Shutterstock, Inc.; page 18, ©Picture Contact/Alamy; page 22, ©Jin Yong/Shutterstock, Inc.; page 23,
©iStockphoto.com/sack; page 24, ©Goto Sayuri/Alamy; page 25, ©Kirk Treakle/Alamy; page 28, ©Photo
Japan/Alamy; page 29, ©mikecranephotography.com/Alamy; page 30, ©Radu Razvan/Shutterstock,
Inc.; page 34, ©Neil Setchfield/Alamy; page 36, ©kevin connors/Shutterstock, Inc.; page 37, ©robert
paul van beets/Shutterstock, Inc.; page 38, ©Kheng Guan Toh/Shutterstock, Inc.; page 40 left, ©Dropu/
Shutterstock, Inc.; page 40 right, ©mashe/Shutterstock, Inc.; page 41, ©David P. Smith/Shutterstock, Inc.;
page 42, ©Joerg Beuge/Shutterstock, Inc.; page 44, ©Liz Van Steenburgh/Shutterstock, Inc.; page 45,
©Muellek Josef/Shutterstock, Inc.

Library of Congress Cataloging-in-Publication Data
Somervill, Barbara A.
  It's cool to learn about countries: Japan/by Barbara A. Somervill.
    p. cm.—(Social studies explorer)
  Includes index.
  ISBN-13: 978-1-60279-832-8 (lib. bdg.)
  ISBN-10: 1-60279-832-X (lib. bdg.)
  1. Japan—Juvenile literature. I. Title. II. Title: Japan. III. Series.
  DS806.S574 2011
  952—dc22                                    2009048894

Cherry Lake Publishing would like to acknowledge the work of The Partnership for
21st Century Skills. Please visit www.21stcenturyskills.org for more information.

Printed in the United States of America
Corporate Graphics Inc.
July 2010
CLFA07

# TABLE OF CONTENTS

# CHAPTER ONE

# WELCOME TO JAPAN!

➥ Are you ready to explore Japan?

It is springtime in Japan. The cherry blossoms paint parks and gardens with shades of soft pink. In a few months, the hot summer sun will send Japanese people to the shores. Japan has 18,486 miles (29,751 kilometers) of coastline. There, they'll enjoy activities such as

swimming and sailing. Autumn's red and golden leaves bring hikers to Japan's many mountains. When winter comes, many take part in ice-skating and skiing.

Pack an *obento*, or Japanese picnic lunch. Then take in Tokyo's attractions. Some include the National Children's Castle and Tokyo Metropolitan Children's Hall. Be sure to tour Tokyo's Pokémon Center, where video games, cartoons, and movies entertain young and old alike.

➥ Japan is rich with interesting culture and history.

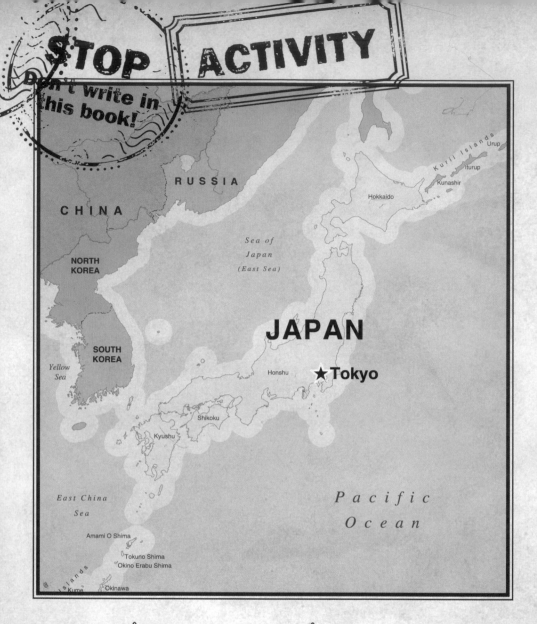

Place a piece of paper over the map of Japan and trace the country's borders. Japan's four major islands are Honshu, Hokkaido, Kyushu, and Shikoku. There are also many smaller islands. One group of these islands is often referred to as the Ryukyu Islands. Use an atlas to find this group of small islands. Label them on your map. Use a star to represent Tokyo, Japan's capital.

Japan measures 145,914 square miles (377,915 square kilometers). That is a bit smaller than the state of California. Japan is a string of islands that stretches approximately 1,500 miles (2,414 km). The largest island is Honshu. Japan's largest cities are found on Honshu. These include Hiroshima, Kobe, Kyoto, Osaka, Nagoya, and Yokohama. Japan's capital city of Tokyo is found on Honshu, too.

◆ Osaka is just one of Japan's many large, modern cities.

The country is surrounded by water. To the east is the Pacific Ocean. To the west is the Sea of Japan. To the west across the Sea of Japan lie South Korea, North Korea, and Russia.

Japan's islands stretch in a line along the coast of Asia.

Mount Fuji, called Fuji-san, is a volcanic mountain. It has not erupted since 1707. Snowcapped Fuji is open to mountain climbing during July and August. It is also the site of Hakone, a nearby hot spring.

Mountains cover most of the country. That is no surprise because volcanic eruptions formed the landscape. Japan has 108 active volcanoes that are constantly monitored for the safety of the Japanese people. Japan experiences approximately 1,500 earthquake **tremors** yearly. Children practice earthquake safety drills in school. Tokyo holds an annual earthquake readiness drill.

In August 2009, a powerful earthquake shook houses in Tokyo and the surrounding area. The 6.4-magnitude earthquake caused building damage, highway closures, and train delays.

Much of Japan enjoys a **temperate** climate with four seasons. In the north, winter is cold with plenty of snow in the mountains. In southern Japan, the winters are milder. Japan has a rainy season that lasts approximately 40 days during the summer months of June and July. Average yearly **precipitation** for most of Japan is approximately 50 inches (1,270 millimeters). Average temperatures in Tokyo range from 38.5 degrees Fahrenheit (3.6 degrees Celsius) in January to 76.5 degrees Fahrenheit (24.7 degrees C) in July.

Japan has a large population for a country its size. This creates serious demands on the environment. Water use is high. Both human and industrial waste pollute the water supply. Land use for housing, business, and agriculture means loss of habitat for native plants and animals. These issues threaten the well-being of Japan's wildlife. The country, fortunately, has taken many steps to help reduce these problems.

The Japanese macaque, or snow monkey, has adjusted well to Japan's cold winters. When the macaques need to warm up, they take dips in hot springs. The population of these clever monkeys is declining. They are losing habitat. They are also killed because they raid local farms for food.

Japan has 24 **endangered** and 15 vulnerable animal species. These include many types of bats, rodents, and whales. Japan has blue, fin, humpback, and other whales swimming in its waters. Japan harvests specific whales for scientific study. The meat from harvested whales sometimes ends up for sale in Japanese supermarkets.

An average humpback whale is between 40 and 50 feet (12 and 15 meters) long and weighs about 40 tons.

# BUSINESS AND GOVERNMENT IN JAPAN

➥ Consumer electronics are a major part of the Japanese economy.

Televisions, sound systems, computers, cars, and cameras. These high-tech products and others are the basis of Japan's economy. Over the past 60 years, Japan's government and industry have worked hard to build a strong economy. Today, Japan is a leading producer of electronic equipment.

More than 4 percent of the population works in agriculture. Nearly 28 percent of workers are involved in industry. More than 66 percent of employees work in services. People with jobs related to industry produce goods for sale. Service workers provide services instead of goods.

The Shinkansen, or bullet train, is a group of high-speed express trains. They move at speeds of up to 186.4 miles (300 kilometers) per hour. This is one of the fastest and cleanest train systems in the world. Thousands of Japanese people travel to and from work on the Shinkansen daily.

Shinkansen

● Japan's farmers grow large amounts of rice.

Besides electronics and computers, Japan's factories turn out textiles. They also produce farm equipment and machine tools. They make steel and other metal products. Japanese brands of motorcycles, cars, trucks, and ships are sold worldwide. Many of these products are **exported** to other countries. Japan's major trading partners include China, the United States, South Korea, Hong Kong, Taiwan, and the European Union.

Agricultural workers produce rice, sugar beets, vegetables, pork, poultry, and dairy products. Fishing is a major industry. Japan has one of the largest fishing fleets in the world. Japanese fishers account for 15 percent of the global fishing catch.

The currency of Japan is called the yen. There are bills for 10,000 yen, 5,000 yen, 2,000 yen, and 1,000 yen. The Japanese use coins for 500 yen, 100 yen, 50 yen, 10 yen, 5 yen, and 1 yen. In 2010, one U.S. dollar equaled approximately 90.6 yen.

Japan catches most of its own fish and grows most of its own rice. Even so, the country must **import** many food products. The nation has few mineral resources. It must also import coal, oil, lumber, and other raw materials.

IMPORT
EXPORT

Do you want to know more about Japan's economy? Take a look at its trading partners. Trading partners are the countries that import goods from a country or export goods to that country. Here is a graph showing the countries that are Japan's top import and export trading partners.

EXPORTS ←— JAPAN ←— IMPORTS

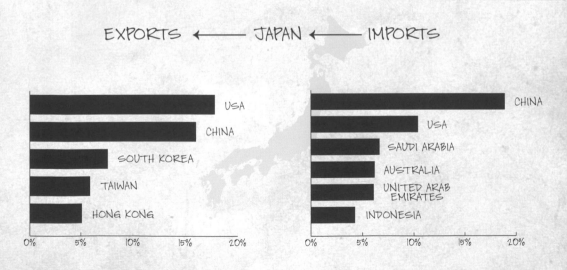

The governing body of Japan is a **parliament**. The head of government is the prime minister. Yukio Hatoyama was elected prime minister in 2009.

The Japanese flag is a white banner with a red circle in the center. The circle represents the sun. The flag is called Hinomaru, or "circle of the sun."

"Kimiqayo" is the Japanese national anthem. It promotes peace and success. The song traces its origin to a waka, a traditional song-poem written in the 10th century. See below for the lyrics and their translation. Then learn how to sing "Kimiqayo." With an adult, look online for sound clips of the anthem for help with the tune and pronunciation.

## Kimiqayo

Words: Anonymous
Music: Hiromori Hayashi

Ki mi qa — yo — wa   chi yo ni — —  ya chi yo ni  sa za re

i shi no  i wa o lo na ri te  Ko ke no  mu — su — ma — — de

| JAPANESE LYRICS | ENGLISH TRANSLATION |
|---|---|
| Kimiqayo wa | Thousands of years of |
| Chiyo ni yachiyo ni | happy reign be thine; |
| Sazareishi no | Rule on, my lord, till what |
| Iwao to narite | are pebbles now |
| Koke no musu made | By ages united to mighty |
| | rocks shall grow |
| | Whose venerable sides the |
| | moss doth line. |

The National Diet has two houses. It is Japan's law-making body. The House of Councillors (*Sangi-in*) has 242 members. They are elected for 6-year terms. The House of Representatives (*Shugi-in*) has 480 seats. Members are elected to serve 4-year terms. At any time, the prime minister and Cabinet can decide to dissolve the House of Representatives and hold a new election.

↩ The Diet holds meetings to discuss new laws for the country.

•► Emperor Akihito is a descendent of Japan's very first emperor.

The official chief of state in Japan is an emperor. Emperors ruled Japan from 660 BCE until after World War II (1939–1945). At that time, the constitution of Japan limited the powers of the emperor to those of a **figurehead**. The current emperor is Emperor Akihito, who rose to the throne in 1989. Akihito has no role in the government, although the Japanese people honor him as their traditional leader.

# CHAPTER THREE

# MEET THE PEOPLE

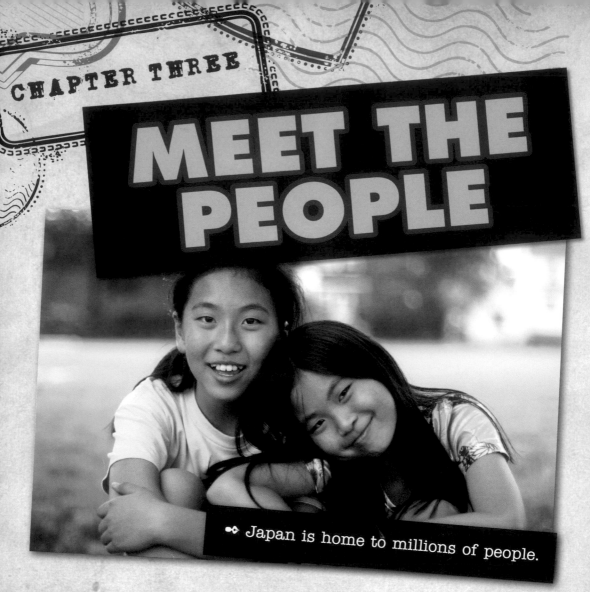

◄ Japan is home to millions of people.

Japan boasts the 10th largest population in the world, even though the country is smaller in size than California. In 2009, the population stood at 127,078,679. That year, it was estimated that the population is declining by more than one-tenth of 1 percent yearly. The country has one of the world's lowest birth rates, as families decide to have fewer children. At the same time, an important part of the population is aging.

Two-thirds of Japan's people live in **urban** areas. The largest city is Tokyo, with more than 12 million people, followed by Yokohama, Osaka, and Nagoya. Most cities are along the coast. They have large harbors and extensive shipping. The metropolitan area of Tokyo and Yokohama plus surrounding suburbs boasts 35 million people.

Japan has a very low rate of immigration. Strict rules prevent people from foreign countries from moving permanently to Japan. As a result, Japan's population is 98.5 percent Japanese. Another 0.5 percent is Korean and 0.4 percent is Chinese.

Tokyo's Shibuya Crossing is known as one of the busiest intersections in the world.

The main language spoken in Japan is Japanese. Most children also learn English in school. Japanese uses characters that represent words or combinations of words. One style of script is called *kanji*. Through the centuries, the number of characters increased so much that learning Japanese became very difficult. Today, the government has an official list of approximately 2,000 characters. Children learn approximately 1,000 kanji characters in elementary school and the rest in middle school.

◆► Japanese students study hard to master every kanji.

◦• Many different subjects are taught in the Japanese school system.

School life consists of 6 years of elementary school, 3 years of middle school, and 3 years of high school. Sixth-graders study science, math, Japanese, physical education, social studies, and other subjects. Students also study music, art, crafts, and English. Learning computer skills is also important. In addition to class work, Japanese students are also responsible for cleaning their classrooms, halls, and schoolyards.

Origami is the art of paper folding. Try making an origami dog's head.

## MATERIALS

- 1 square of brown construction paper, 8 inches (20.3 centimeters) by 8 inches (20.3 cm)
- Black marker

## INSTRUCTIONS

1. Working on a flat surface, fold the square of paper diagonally to form a triangle.

2. Pretend the triangle is an arrowhead. The arrow should be pointing towards you. Fold the point that is closest to you back. This creates a flat chin for the dog.

3. Fold the left-hand and right-hand points of the triangle down. This forms the dog's ears.

STEP ONE

STEP TWO

STEP THREE

4. Depending on the angles of the folds you created in Step #3, there may or may not be a point at the top of the dog's head. If there is, fold this top point away from you. This creates a flat head for the dog.

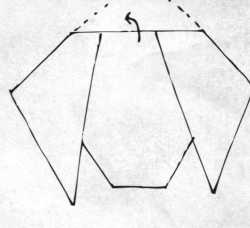

5. Using a marker, draw eyes and a nose on the dog's face.

Try making several versions with different sizes and colors of paper.

➤ Martial arts are popular among people of all ages.

Uniforms are required for most middle school and high school students. Girls wear skirts and special shirts. Boys wear pants, white shirts, and jackets.

Students are active in sports, both in school and out. Most schools have sports teams. Jujitsu and other martial arts are popular after-school activities. Students also visit museums and attend theater or traditional dance presentations. Children can also join clubs.

Sumo wrestling is a major sport in Japan. Sumo dates back more than 1,000 years. The rules of sumo are very simple. Two wrestlers meet in a ring that is 15 feet (4.6 meters) in diameter. Some wrestlers weigh more than 440 pounds (200 kilograms). They slam into each other, pushing the opponent toward the ring's edge. When a wrestler steps out of the ring or touches the floor with anything but his feet, he loses. There are six championship sumo tournaments each year. Victorious sumo wrestlers are honored heroes.

➥ Few sports are as popular in Japan as sumo wrestling.

# CHAPTER FOUR

# CELEBRATIONS

➥ The Aoba Matsuri Festival is held each spring in the city of Sendai.

Japan honors its rich heritage by celebrating several national and religious holidays. January 1 is New Year's Day. This is a day to wish friends and relatives good luck in the coming year. The Japanese send special greeting cards called *nengajo* for New Year's. At midnight after New Year's Eve, people gather at the local Buddhist temple to hear the temple bell rung 108 times. This number is special to Buddhists, as they believe it chases evil away for the year.

# HOLIDAYS

These are some holidays that are recognized in Japan

| | |
|---|---|
| January 1 | New Year's Day |
| Second Monday of January | Coming of Age Day |
| February 11 | National Foundation Day |
| March 20 or 21 | Spring Equinox |
| April 29 | Showa Day |
| May 3 | Constitution Memorial Day |
| May 4 | Greenery Day |
| May 5 | Children's Day |
| Third Monday of July | Ocean Day |
| Third Monday of September | Respect for the Aged Day |
| September 23 or 24 | Autumn Equinox |
| Second Monday of October | Health and Sports Day |
| November 3 | Culture Day |
| November 23 | Labor Thanksgiving Day |
| December 23 | Emperor's Birthday |

Throughout the year, the Japanese celebrate the changing of seasons. Respect for nature is part of the Shinto religion. *Setsubun*, celebrated on February 3, announces the arrival of spring. In March, the spring equinox is a national holiday. The fall equinox is celebrated in late September. On these days, people visit the graves of relatives.

# CRAFT ACTIVITY

Japanese families fly carp-shaped kites as part of Children's Day celebrations. How about making your own?

## MATERIALS

- Large sheets of white paper
- Tape
- Crayons
- Craft wire
- Wire cutters
- 2 feet (0.6 m) string
- Ruler
- Scissors

## INSTRUCTIONS

1. Draw a fish shape on a piece of white paper. The fish should be 12 inches (30.5 cm) long, 4 inches (10.2 cm) wide at the body, and 6 inches (15.2 cm) wide at the tail. The mouth should be 2 inches (5.1 cm) wide. Use a ruler to measure these dimensions. Draw a separate fin. Cut out the fin and fish shapes.
2. Repeat Step #1 to create the other side of the fish and a second fin.
3. Tape both sides of the fish together along the edges. Leave the mouth and the end of the tail open. Tape one fin onto each side of the fish.

4. Color your fish kite with crayons.
5. Use scissors to make cuts around the fish's mouth. The cuts should be 0.25 inches (0.6 cm) long and spaced 0.25 inches (0.6 cm) apart.
6. Use craft wire and wire cutters to carefully form a circle that is 1.25 inches (3.2 cm) in diameter.
7. Place this wire ring just inside the fish's mouth. Bend the paper tabs over the wire ring. Tape the tabs in place. This should keep the fish's mouth open.
8. Tape the ends of the string to each side of the fish's mouth.

Grab the string and have fun making the fish swim and dance through the air.

❧ Parades and performances are held during Golden Week.

The entire nation closes down to celebrate Golden Week. It lasts from April 29 through May 5. April 29 is Showa Day. May 3 is Constitution Memorial Day. It honors the day when the new Japanese constitution became effective after World War II. May 4 is Greenery Day, honoring Emperor Showa's love for plants. May 5 is Children's Day, when parents fly carp kites in their children's honor.

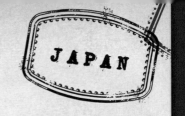
# ZODIAC

The Japanese zodiac calendar is made up of a 12-year cycle. Each year in the calendar cycle is represented by a different animal. Children born under an animal's sign are believed to take on certain characteristics. A child born in the year of the rat, for example, should be clever, creative, and hard working.

| 2010 | Year of the Tiger | 2016 | Year of the Monkey |
| 2011 | Year of the Rabbit | 2017 | Year of the Rooster |
| 2012 | Year of the Dragon | 2018 | Year of the Dog |
| 2013 | Year of the Snake | 2019 | Year of the Boar |
| 2014 | Year of the Horse | 2020 | Year of the Rat |
| 2015 | Year of the Sheep | 2021 | Year of the Ox |

Religious holidays are times for prayer, fasting, or honoring one's **ancestors**. Slightly more than 80 percent of Japanese people follow Shintoism. Seventy-one percent follow Buddhism. These numbers add up to more than 100 percent because many people belong to both religions. *Shinto* means "the way of the gods." Shintoism blends ancient Japanese traditions with respect for

❧ The Heian shrine in Kyoto is a well-known Shinto shrine.

⇒ Buddha statues are a common sight in Japanese gardens.

nature, ancestors, and spirits. Japanese spring and autumn festivals are Shinto celebrations. Buddhists follow the teachings of Siddhartha Gautama, called the Buddha. Buddhism encourages followers to live moral lives, to be aware of their thoughts and actions, and to seek wisdom. There are also small numbers of Christians and followers of other religions in Japan.

# CHAPTER FIVE

# WHAT'S FOR DINNER?

➡ Mochi is just one of the delicious treats Japanese cuisine has to offer.

The main food at every Japanese meal has historically been rice. Steamed rice is eaten at breakfast, lunch, and dinner. *Mochi* (rice cakes) are eaten as snacks. Each person gets a bowl of rice at lunch or dinner and adds meat or vegetables to it.

A traditional Japanese breakfast includes rice, miso soup, and side dishes. Typical side dishes include grilled fish, pickles, or dried *nori* (seaweed). Lunch is either rice or noodles in soup. People often bring a lunch box to school or work. Rice balls, sushi rolls, and steamed rice are commonly packed for lunch. Dinner is the main meal of the day.

Japanese people eat with chopsticks called hashi. Japanese chopsticks can be made from bamboo, plastic, wood, or metal and are pointed on the end.

The Japanese have several styles of preparing foods. Sushi and sashimi are ways of serving raw fish. Tempura meats and vegetables are battered and deep-fried. Green beans, fish, and sweet potatoes are some popular foods served tempura-style.

Sushi and sashimi are very popular. Sushi is finger-sized pieces of raw fish, vegetables, and rice. Sashimi is raw fish that is sliced very thin and served without rice.

sushi

sashimi

➥ Stir fried meat and vegetables are usually served over a bed of rice.

Cooking on a grill is common. Hibachi grilling requires cooking over hot coals. Teppanyaki cooking involves grilling meat or fish on a very hot iron plate. Meat, fish, and vegetables are stir-fried and seasoned with soy sauce or teriyaki sauce. Meats include beef, pork, and chicken. Seafood includes shrimp and tuna. Vegetables include mung bean sprouts, cabbage, spinach, **daikon**, turnips, **taro root**, and carrots. These foods are served with rice or noodles.

For seasoning, cooks use fresh ginger, soy sauce, and teriyaki sauce. They also use *mirin*, *miso*, *komesu*, and *wasabi*. Mirin is a sweet wine used for cooking. Miso is a soybean paste commonly found in soup. Komesu is the rice vinegar used in sushi dishes. For an extra kick, people add *wasabi*. It is an exceptionally hot and spicy horseradish.

❖ Ginger is a flavorful root that is usually ground up or thinly sliced.

# ACTIVITY RECIPE

Try this recipe for teriyaki vegetables. This dish requires chopping vegetables and working with hot oil over a stovetop. Be sure to ask an adult for help.

## Teriyaki Vegetables

INGREDIENTS

1 small onion, peeled

1 zucchini

1 carrot

salt and pepper

2 tablespoons (30 milliliters) cooking oil

¼ cup (59 ml) teriyaki sauce

Instructions are on the following page →

1. Rinse the zucchini and carrot. Clean the carrot with a vegetable peeler.

2. Have an adult slice the onion into very thin pieces. Next, he or she should slice the zucchini on an angle into thin pieces. The carrot should be sliced thinly, too.

3. Have an adult heat the skillet over medium-high heat. Carefully add the oil.

4. When the oil is hot, stir-fry the vegetables until the onions and zucchini are golden brown. Use tongs to stir everything.

5. Sprinkle lightly with salt and pepper.

6. Add the teriyaki sauce and stir well.

A great way to serve these vegetables is over rice. Give it a try!

◆ You can try this recipe with almost any combination of vegetables and meat.

◆ Noodle soups are a favorite food for Japanese people looking for a quick, simple meal.

Japanese people enjoy a variety of ethnic foods when they eat out. Large cities have restaurants offering everything from pizza to fish and chips. Japanese diners can enjoy Italian pasta, French stews, fried chicken, and cheeseburgers. For those who prefer home-style cooking, there are noodle booths and shops that specialize in rice.

Japan is a nation that blends the traditional with the modern. What part of this exciting country will you explore next?

# GLOSSARY

**ancestors** (AN-sess-turz) people from whom one is descended

**daikon** (DIE-kun) a large, white radish

**endangered** (en-DAYN-jurd) at risk of dying out completely

**equinox** (EE-kwih-noks) one of two days in the year when day and night are the same length of time

**exported** (EK-spor-tid) sent something to another country to be sold there

**figurehead** (FIG-yur-hed) a person who has an important position but no power

**import** (IM-port) bring in from another country

**magnitude** (MAG-nih-tood) the measured power of an earthquake

**parliament** (PAR-luh-mehnt) the lawmaking body of certain countries

**precipitation** (prih-sip-ih-TAY-shuhn) the total amount of rain, hail, sleet, snow, or ice that falls from the sky

**taro root** (TAR-oh ROOT) a starchy potato-like vegetable that is the large edible underground stem of the taro plant

**temperate** (TEM-pur-it) having neither very low nor very high temperatures

**tremors** (TREM-urz) vibrating or shaking movements

**urban** (UR-buhn) having to do with cities

# FOR MORE INFORMATION

## Books

Goulding, Sylvia. *Festive Foods! Japan*. New York: Chelsea Clubhouse, 2008.

Kalman, Bobbie. *Japan: The Culture*. New York: Crabtree Publishing, 2009.

Phillips, Charles. *Japan*. Washington, DC: National Geographic, 2007.

## Web Sites

**Kids Web Japan**
*web-japan.org/kidsweb/*
Learn about Japanese culture and more at this resource.

**National Geographic Kids—Japan**
*kids.nationalgeographic.com/Places/Find/Japan*
Find many facts about Japan at this helpful site.

**TIME for Kids—Japan**
*www.timeforkids.com/TFK/kids/hh/goplaces/ main/0,28375,555016,00.html*
Explore information about Japan's history and more at this interesting site.

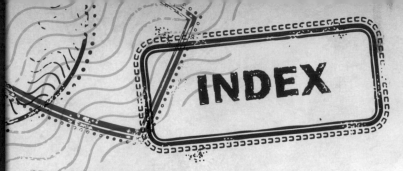

# INDEX

ABOUT THE AUTHOR
Barbara Somervill has never been to Japan, but she loves Japanese food, arts and crafts, and haiku. Barbara has written about many different countries and has a never-ending list of places she hopes to visit. Japan is at the top of the list.